BEES

P9-BZW-289

Created by Gallimard Jeunesse,
Ute Fuhr, and Raoul Sautai
Illustrated by Ute Fuhr and
Raoul Sautai

A FIRST DISCOVERY BOOK

SCHOLASTIC INC.

New York   Toronto   London   Auckland   Sydney

What is that bee doing
behind the flower?

Here are the members
of the bee family.

Worker bee   Queen   Drone

It is feeding on
nectar and collecting pollen
to make honey.

Some bees
create a kind of glue,
called propolis, from plant
gums and resins.
They use it to seal
cracks in the walls
of their beehive.

Look closely at the
head of a bee.

It sees, moves around, and communicates
with other bees by using its eyes,
which are on opposite sides of its head,
and its antennae.

The antennae
allow them to recognize the scent of other bees.

When the bee has found a field of flowers, it figures out where it is
by comparing the distance between the sun and its beehive.

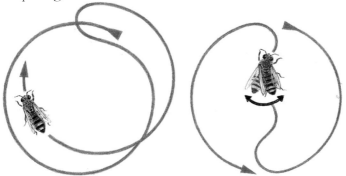

By flying in circles, it signals to other bees
the direction and the distance to the flowers it has found.

In order to eat, bees leave the beehive
in search of nectar and pollen.
Then they return to hives
like the wooden one here.

The youngest bees do the housecleaning, stock up the food, feed the larvae, and keep an eye on the front door.

By flapping their wings, the bees keep the air in their beehive cool.

How is the beehive made?

The bee eats honey...

...and its body turns it into wax. It pulls the wax out of its abdomen with its feet.

The worker bees make
wax scales, which they chew
and soften with their jaws.
Then they stick them together
to make the cells you see here.

When the queen goes on a mating flight,
hundreds of drones pursue her.
She chooses about ten drones to mate with.

Then the queen enters the hive to lay her eggs.

Workers surround the queen as she lays one egg in each cell. She can lay over 1,000 eggs a day!

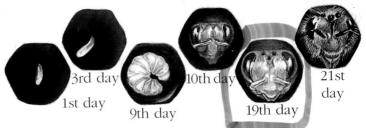

3rd day

1st day

9th day

10th day

19th day

21st day

After eight days, the worker bees close the cells with a wax cover.

When the young bee emerges from its cell, a worker bee gives it nectar to drink.

The queen, thousands of workers, and some drones fly out of the hive. This is called swarming.

What happens when there is no more room in the beehive?

The swarm gathers
together and flies
to a nearby branch
to wait while
scout bees search
for a new home.

32

A couple of days later
the bees are settled
in their new hive.

Beehives
can take
different
forms.

Here are some of the tools of a beekeeper.

  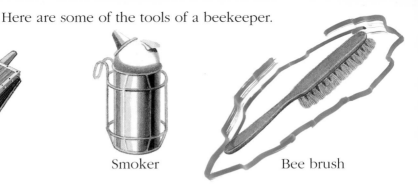

Bellows   Smoker   Bee brush

At the end of the summer the beekeeper
takes a frame full of honey from the beehive.
Then with his knife, he scrapes the honey
off the comb.

Each honey tastes slightly different,
depending on which flowers
the nectar came from.

Winter has come and the bees slow down and rest, or hibernate, inside their hive. The bees cluster and keep close to their queen. They feed themselves with the honey that they stored during the summer.

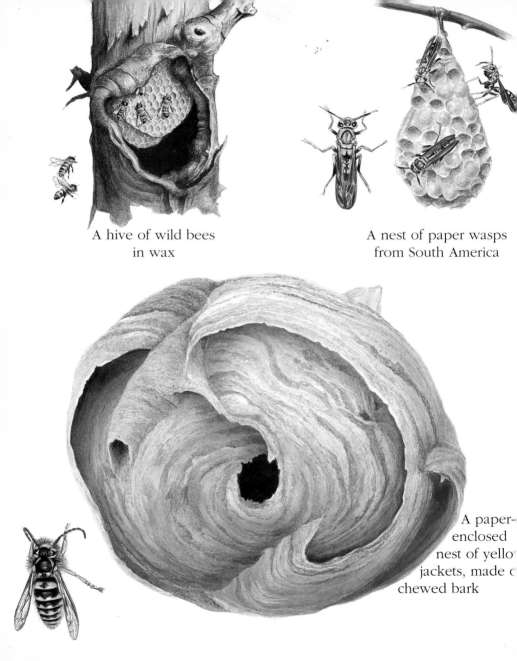

A hive of wild bees
in wax

A nest of paper wasps
from South America

A paper-
enclosed
nest of yello
jackets, made c
chewed bark

The work of other insect master builders!

South
American
wasp nest made
from vegetable fibers
that have been flattened
down into a paste

One of the most unbelievable
insect-made buildings is the
termite mound.

It is built
out of soil
and saliva.

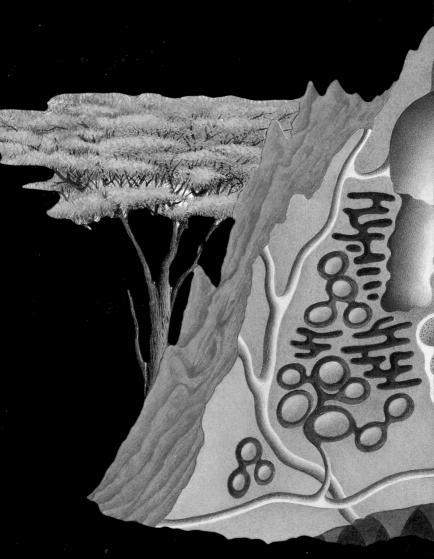

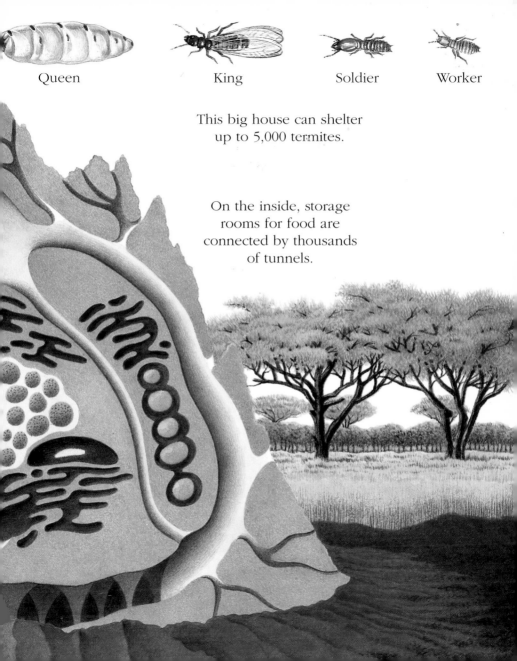

Queen

King

Soldier

Worker

This big house can shelter
up to 5,000 termites.

On the inside, storage
rooms for food are
connected by thousands
of tunnels.

Library of Congress Cataloging-in-Publication Data available.

Originally published in France under the title *L'abeille* by Editions Gallimard Jeunesse.

No part of this publication may be reproduced in whole or in part, or stored in a retrieval system, c
transmitted in any form or by any means, electronic, mechanical, photocopying, recording, c
otherwise, without written permission of the publisher. For information regarding permission, write
Scholastic Inc., 555 Broadway, New York, NY 10012.

ISBN 0-590-93780-4

Copyright © 1992 by Editions Gallimard Jeunesse.
This edition English translation by Heather Miller.
This edition American text by Wendy Barish.
This edition Expert Reader: Professor Whitney S. Cranshaw, Department of Entomology,
Colorado State University
All rights reserved. Published by Scholastic Inc., 555 Broadway, New York, NY 10012, by arrangeme
with Editions Gallimard Jeunesse, 5 rue Sebastien-Bottin, F-75007, Paris, France.

SCHOLASTIC and A FIRST DISCOVERY BOOK and associated logos are trademarks and/or registered
trademarks of Scholastic Inc.
12 11 10 9 8 7 6 5 4 3 2   8 9/9 0 1/0
Printed in Italy by Editoriale Libraria
First Scholastic printing, March 1997